Retail Park

Samuel Millar

Retail Park

QUERENCIA

Querencia Press, LLC
Chicago Illinois

QUERENCIA PRESS

© Copyright 2022
Samuel Millar

LIBRARY OF CONGRESS CATALOG-IN-PUBLICATION DATA

ISBN 979 8 9860788 2 3

www.querenciapress.com

First Published in 2022

Querencia Press, LLC
Chicago IL

Printed & Bound in the United States of America

CONTENTS

Foreword & Trigger Warning:

I don't know when the first full draft of 'Retail Park' was put together, but I know some of the oldest poems in this were written around 6 years ago. I'm not really sure if that's a long time anymore but I never would've thought back then that they would be published, and I still can't wrap my head round it now. I'm so thankful to be in this position and I hope you enjoy these poems and take anything you need from them.

This collection explores themes that include self-harm and religion as well as descriptions of blood.

For Caron, the perfect teacher

this isn't how everyone does it

I've got you

Caught his jaw, fizzing
hands like hammers
playful press presence
and dismissal of praise after the day is saved,
I thought
I'd always feel this good

I could save a bank in the time it takes
for you to draw the gun,
catch a bullet between my fingers and fire it back
just under the knee,
I'll find the killer
from the way they cut the throat
and filter the thoughts of everyone who hopes
to do the worst they can

I'll be asked to drain the rivers,
speak at your birthdays,
find your keys,
and I want to,
I really want to,
but some days are too short

I didn't take you on as a sidekick,
apprentice, or confidant
I just needed someone else to see,
and maybe when I'm older
you'll take all the parts they thought the best,
do something with them

I fly through the wall
and catch my cape on the door,
snap back,
not my first mistake,

but it's different now

overpowered, your leg is caught under rubble
and you're crawling,
to turn your body would mean looking away,
and you've never done that

I've got your eyes and I hold them,
what happens next
won't fix anything,
but I couldn't keep it up,
the pressure
from forearm clasping hand
around neck and squeeze,

I say,
"I want this,"
don't let that torture you,
no more room in my mouth for an explanation
I collapse to the sound
of your one scream, amplified

I wasn't here to let you down today,
and I hope you made it out,

I'm sorry I couldn't do that first

Some sick lesson

I go home, whistling
sometimes sirens
sometimes birds
and when I wake up
there is no day I've repeated
always different
sometimes dangerous

if meeting you was an accident
that's okay
mistakes are always made
but when you leave
I don't know if I can teach
like you
how to detach
one burnt building
one stranger screaming
one pint of blood spilled

remember weekends on top of buildings
our ears to the ground
not hoping for something to fly to
but ready
I've had my hand held willingly
not ready to leave the comfort
of your outstretched arm

that made it easy
for me to be caught
and for you to come find me
when I wake I'm cuffed
beyond my ability to break
I hear your whistling
then thunder through the door

head first

first thought is natural
You've never truly needed my help
willing spectator and friend
second thought is different
you've not stuck the landing
and now your head is in their hands

and I'm crying
building collapsing under the weight of your entrance
I'm stuck
hands tied and legs caught
I'll watch you until the rivers dry
because you know how best to keep going

and you look to me
"I want this"
your body twists out of sync
with your neck
and you fall
ear to the ground

but I didn't get to say goodbye

Bricks

when people talk about us
they'll say we were born for this
that every part of me is appalled
by every part of you

I only ever wanted to do this
to know I could

take something that eclipses
all I've ever known
and crush it
ant-hill under boot

There's no grand plan
outside of taking your friend
from their walk home
I just need to know you're coming

I'm only waiting minutes
and there you are
and as wrong as it is
to capitalize on your mistake
it seems it was meant to be
your upturned head
my crushing arms

I was expecting something different
I thought you'd throw me into the future
with one thrust of your hand
no
maybe my time moved quicker
than it took for you to realize
something's gone wrong
I'll never know

but I did it

now what

keeping clean

Jesus is coming, look busy

We anticipate
bread, bathed
in thousand island dressing
and lettuce leaves,
fresh from Dad's fingers

who will send the year's prayer forward?
I'd become so good
at being thankful,
but left
with nothing to say,
choking,
without a joke
or respect
for our years together,
Ben speaks
future theologian
a history between God
and the dining room,
hands squeeze in canon,
we open
eyes and stomachs,
exchange plates
and salt shakers,
look towards the skylight
hope someone listened

Saint Benjamin

Come home, tell me
what did you learn today
and what did you sing?
I took to miming
because I didn't like the volume
of high notes and competition.

Peace be with you
and also with you

you were always so good at intercessions,
young enough to be hopeful
before you leave to learn
the history of God

There's a baptism on Sunday,
booked today in haste,
her baby almost died
and she wanted to know
he'd be safe

What promises did you make?

I told her
what we both needed
we'll always be here
when it gets difficult

I know you're not trained to listen,
but you're good
without trying
don't lose that

Goodbye Benjamin

the kindness is gone
so long feeling he's drained
from table talk and strangers
didn't offer to carry a man on his back
hasn't stopped thinking about it
might think this means he cares more
is hiding it in the face of dismissive
and argumentative
but no
said he doesn't want to wake up caring anymore
let it die
let it all
crushed by the weight of strangeness
who am I if not the things I give you
no more
time, you think
might be better spent in cynicism
but I don't think that's you
and I hope it never is
prove me right
selfish to measure the good in the world
against the way you treat it
don't let me down Ben
you always have more to give

keep it ticking

On the long road home we got very, very lost

offered his body as a bridge when faced with
an impossibly long step
tested out electric fences with his teeth
to avoid tragedy
wrapped his shirt around his fist
to get through windows
only ever wanting to spare us the danger in knocking
did his best, always tried
and did his best
if he hadn't lost his tongue
keeping us fed
he'd say he'd give his heartbeat
to do it all again

I'll take that

Hard skin strips
the sides of your fingers
the same place I bite myself
calluses
like bubbles

fingernails
stained aluminum
and breath
still washing
strangers with a need to please
I'll take that part from you
obsessively
scared everyone would leave
echoed when I can't take the bus
but you stayed
when your dad didn't
small pieces you broke away
and changed
your mum used children's nails
to scratch scabs
you told us stories instead
I'll take
love and humor
cooking and clean shirts
unconditional
desire to help
and leave the things
we keep between us
heads smashed into kitchen cupboards
armchair silence
and addiction
a love of
something to hide

will it work
my turn to tell you
wait and see

it's not how we thought it'd go

That wasn't fair on the birds

I'd heard the plan was to give our bodies sparrows bones,
blessed
and crushed to an impossibly small size,
have them poured in the supposedly holy mixture with
knitting needles for scratching,
plans for a temple,
and honeycomb for healing

really, what else could I ask for,
something to help my eyes
and stronger arms for casting off
the secrets for killing body and soul

Pink, like his brain

Like his favourite salmon shirt,
like cheeks changing
hit with the wind,
stepping into the city
pink,
like his knuckles,
and the stream up his fingers
to the tip is pink
and numb
pink, because he's embarrassed
pink, because he's pinched the inside of his wrist,
nervous
pink, when his mum calls him perfect
and pink,
like crushed berries
up the sides of his leg

If this doesn't help, I might be fucked

He's kept a four leaf clover under a cut below the knee
in case of emergency
but has left it to soak in lieu of frantic sliding

replaced the hinges of his jaw with wishbones
but doesn't want to waste their promise
so keeps his mouth closed

keeps crushed ladybird shells in his pocket
like glass shards turning to sand in his fingers
and had his nose broken
protecting his claim to a loose coin taken
by a stranger's boot

so when the time comes
when it really matters
he won't worry

watching you for movement

There are similarities

My mutilated feet
match thighs
taped like boxers' hands
stained
and yours
fall apart with every step
you watch me
age
I'm watching you
rest
the glamour of growing old
was worn from you
so soon

Becoming a Mermaid

Wasn't shocked when you told me the first problem
was your singing voice
and aversion to public performances
and at the start you said you loved
to hear your fishes speak
before they asked for you to set them free or drain the tank
and now you scrape
screaming as scales sit flush against your thigh
cutting up like the jagged rocks you're scared to sit on
dragging yourself to the bathroom
for another long soak
then you say you can't swim
as if I could leave you to struggle finding your new feet
and not pack a slow boat to the middle of the ocean with you
you might lose your voice
and your movement
take long trips to the pool
terrorise locals with your new legend
and only be spotted in grainy corners
of holiday pictures
but it won't change a thing

studying old age

The language of flowers

Surprise
when the plants grow taller than him
kept at the back of the garden
waiting for summer

takes tools
from his shed
an arsenal
stops the wind

cuts grass
tells us
she'll never be the woman she was

trims leaves
tells Dad
his drink is perfect

pulls weeds
tells Mum
she's making herself sick

scratches our throat
keeps us quiet
tell ourselves
one day
he'll be soil

It'll be so much longer now

Draft eases up the back from behind a towel taped across the broken doorframe, put there to stop exactly this. Dad tells us that after dipping her toe in and out of hospitals like she was scared to explore the depths of a great Roman Bath, that Gran is finally scared of where she's going.

the last chance you get
to wallow in the warm mud
and hope for more time

Compounding the fear, he tells us there's no way we'll see her face. No screen in her house will receive us. "She doesn't have the internet," he says, "the last of the last of her generation to still be scared of it."

return to phone calls
after all your many missed
opportunities

Without a timeline we'll only ever be waiting. Looking across to Ben and back, I see their eyes close and shift, settling their mind with a, "peace be with you"

even if I knew
what it was you needed, when
could I hand it over?

Would you look at that

you know
we've never been as old as this
and we've had a pretty good innings
I think
I haven't seen nearly enough
as they told me I would
but where better to be

he says, I know
and as much as we've been avoiding it
it's getting late

you're too early for the good part

Through and out

There was time
now time again
pulled from the edge
of the event horizon
I am outside
ash
and inside
falling
if I haven't gone alone
collect me
with goodbyes and apologies
and take me back
if I've found a world
one step removed
trust it to be better

Nothing more when exhausts engage

This is us for just a little bit longer
before booster and second stage separation
disentangle our hands
with their one million tiny wired fingers
and let us go
this is where I say goodbye
you've got all of space
and I've been prepared for home
computer programmed fear of death
kept on for the fall
to taste the fear of failure
and the excitement
I really wish it could've been me
not you
up there
but there's no time left
this is where rockets smash
and I never see you again
Godspeed

It spins even when you're off it

had a prayer in mind
with thanks for bringing the sun
please don't disappoint

scared of the speed of
an always spinning Earth
I beg to be lifted

it's getting quieter
I feel it pull at my ears
something's changing

it seems as though
it was already perfect
a tough pill to swallow

but you're definitely here

He's either very wrong or didn't get in

Heaven, he thought
is ladles of medicine spooned softly into his mouth from god's
gentle fingers
it's resting on a bed of stacked silk
made for his body and all the ways it warps
knowing that he wasn't right about much but made it anyway

Ever will be

Weight placed
on uneven pavement slabs
and upturned grass patches
from bike riders
and boots slipped from heads into grass
could convince myself of its innocence
if I hadn't heard the crying

forgive abuse
hurled from cars
on appearance
stopped on pathways when you thought
it was quiet
because we're all trying to get it out
and get away

watch roads stretch out
and panic no one else can see it
does the world end from my shoe tip
or the middle of a southeast back road
sandwiched between capital and coast
or is the town enlarged
by what I'm thinking of it

I need you
like patient to drip
feed me sadness
feed me family home
and old friends
reasons to write
and to be scared
and I'll give you company
residency
and the promise

no matter how long I'm away
or how hard I'm trying
I'll always come back

I Built This

Made my cage of brass
a dome
like Victorian taxidermy
never wanted to deep dive
fishes and submarines
never appealed
just wanted to be high
higher than most
wanted shallow breaths
and the feel of clouds between fingers
attached birds to string
and told them
take me up
then take me forward
I wanted to kiss the heels of black sky
from blue
instead I got blisters from welding
and the sound of necks breaking in unison
don't know how I'll explain this one

CPSIA information can be obtained
at www.ICGtesting.com
Printed in the USA
BVHW030859170622
640057BV00014B/291